1 + 1 = 2
Maybe?

1 + 1 = 2 Maybe?

WHAT IF EVERYTHING YOU
THOUGHT YOU KNEW ABOUT
INVESTING WAS WRONG

• • •

Lee Hyder

© 2017 Lee Hyder
All rights reserved.

ISBN: 1541343034
ISBN 13: 9781541343030
Library of Congress Control Number: 2016921557
CreateSpace Independent Publishing Platform
North Charleston, South Carolina

About the Author

• • •

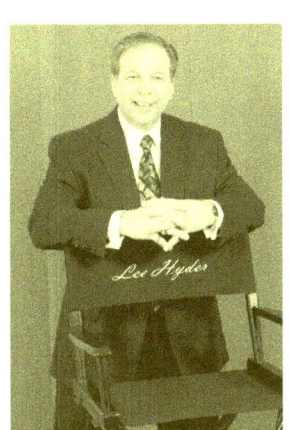

I HAVE BEEN COACHING NORTHEAST Ohio families for almost twenty-five years on how to design financial portfolios that will help them achieve the retirement they have dreamed of one day enjoying. We have taught these very topics and philosophies at many of the local colleges and universities.

In the old days (now I sound like my dad), retirement planning seemed so much easier. For the most part, you didn't need to worry about running out of money during retirement; you had a pension and health insurance. You could count on the company you worked for to take care of you. That has changed for most of us. Today you have to worry about whether you will have a pension when you retire and whether you are doing all the right things with your money to make it last your entire lifetime—and don't get me started about health insurance. Today we have all the crazy Internet websites, talking heads on TV and radio shouting out their endless messages and beliefs that the stock market is predictable.

All you needed to do is whatever they are saying to do with your money, and your financial success is almost assured. Most people today would scoff at a fortune-teller at a county fair who predicted your future. Many people today accept lock, stock, and barrel stock predictions because they come from a well-known TV or radio anchor, website, or magazine.

This so-called objective, impersonal advice is dressed up and packaged as consumer education when it's nothing more than a fancy and expensive infomercial for whatever they are selling today. Sadly, for most investors, I feel the real education they long for comes too late after they bit on the apple and took all this impersonal advice from someone they don't even know. Worse yet, all these advice givers have no idea about your personal situation, wants, financial needs, or risk tolerance.

I can't tell you the countless number of people who would come into my office or called me, wanting to buy something they saw on TV, heard about on the radio, or read somewhere last night. It is amazing the power the TV, radio, and Internet have on people's minds, emotions and investing decisions. I know—not yours!

Emotions can be a wonderful gift, but investing needs to be one human activity we leave our emotions out of. Throughout this book, I hope to identify many of these investing traps that are all around us

1 + 1 = 2 Maybe?

and show you how you can avoid them. Once you recognize them, it will be much easier for you to come up with an investing philosophy and strategy that will help you make better decisions with your investments.

Size Doesn't Matter

• • •

OR AT LEAST THAT'S WHAT my editor said.

This book won't be long because it doesn't have to be to get my simple yet powerful points across to you.

I am going to share with you what I have learned over my twenty-five years of dealing both with portfolios and with the people who have them.

Art Linkletter once said, "Kids say the darndest things." I will take artistic privilege and change that a little by saying "investors" do the darnedest things.

Who will benefit by reading this book?

If you are hoping this book will be full of charts, graphs, technical data, and secret stock tips that will make you rich overnight, you better read every page very carefully because you are already in danger of destroying your future retirement.

Many believe that to be a successful investor and get on track for a great retirement, all you need to do is the following:

1 + 1 = 2 Maybe?

1. Watch TV or listen to a radio show where the host barks out stock tips as casually as a waitress yells to a short-order cook, "Eggs over easy."
2. Subscribe to the newest newsletter promising you the greatest stock tips that can't miss.
3. Ask Google or any other website what's hot.
4. Buy or consider buying some overpriced educational or trading systems.
5. Rely on your custodian's magical online tools and research.
6. Believe that past performance of a mutual fund or stock is a pretty good indicator of how it will perform in the future.
7. Really believe that the stock market is predictable.
8. Belong to an investing club.

9. Rely on Morningstar as the final authority for what to invest in.
10. Or best yet, just invest in whatever your buddy or best friend says he or she does because you think your friend really knows what he or she is doing!

A serious warning about taking well-meaning investing advice from your good friends who, to the outside world, may appear as if they are successful investors and really know what they are doing: They may have the big houses, expensive cars, and memberships to "the club," and they are always taking fun vacations. They seem to have it all. You may secretly even be a little jealous of their lives. *Be very careful what you wish for.*

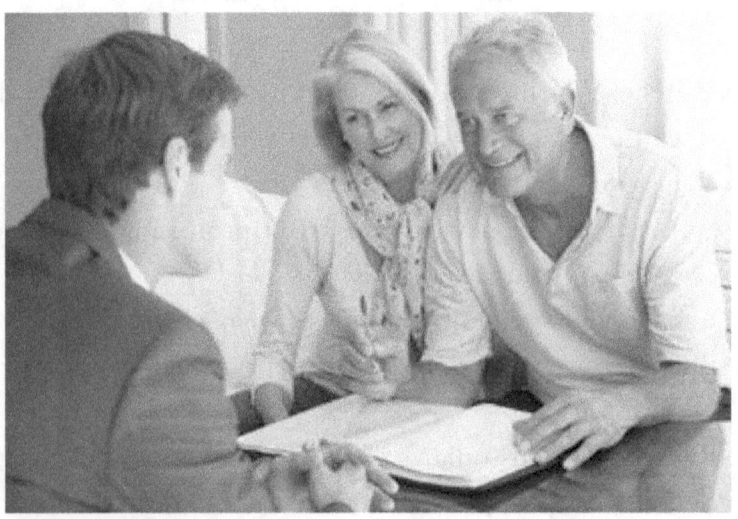

I can't tell you how often I sit in front of a family that looks great to the outside world. They certainly look like they have it all, but after they share with me what's really going on financially, the real picture is much different from the one they portray to everyone else. Even though they came to my office in an expensive car, many of these families are in serious financial trouble and don't even know it. I can't believe how many people walk into my office with $25,000 or more in credit-card debt, have stripped all their equity from their huge, well-manicured home, and have expensive cars with huge payments and even loans against their 401(k)s. The irony of these sad situations is these people tend to be the most opinionated and eager to share their secrets about how you should invest your money in the market. *Please be very careful from whom you take life-changing advice from.*

1 + 1 = 2 Maybe?

• • •

BEING A FINANCIAL ADVISER—SOMEONE WHO has dealt with numbers, math, graphs, charts, and formulas over my entire twenty-five-year professional career—how can I possibly say **1 + 1 = 2 maybe**?

First of all, not only will I demonstrate to you that this is true, but soon you will come to realize, like I have, that our entire economy is based on the simple truth that **1 + 1 = 2 maybe** or, said another way, "sometimes." What I am trying to say is, quite often, what we see with our own eyes and think we understand may actually be more complicated than we realize. The outcome that we believed to be so cut and dried may not be as predictable after all.

I first learned of this well-guarded secret almost fifty-five years ago as a young child sitting around the kitchen table with my family. My father was a CPA. He liked to joke by saying that was an acronym for "cleaning, pressing, and alterations." I didn't think it was funny, but he always smiled when he said it.

I was always intrigued when my father would fill in endless numbers perfectly in column after column with those lead refill pencils that are almost impossible to find today. I remember looking over his shoulder and asking what he was doing. He would try to explain to me in CPA language that it was his job to try to help families reduce the amount of income tax they owed. I would ask this: If they owed it, how can you save them any money? That idea was foreign to this nine-year-old boy. Even I knew you owe what you owe.

As a nine-year-old, I needed a much simpler explanation, so my dad shared with me his secret formula: **$1 + 1 = 2$ maybe** or sometimes.

Not only would this simple mathematical example stay with me my entire life, but it would become a foundational belief that guided me in helping countless people achieve peace of mind as investors and, more importantly, help them better understand the world they live in. I guess what my dad was simply trying to say to me was that things may really not be as cut and dried as they appear to be.

Are you ready to learn this formula and see how it can affect your entire life?

Okay, here it is.

$$u+v)u+(-u+v)y+(5u+2v)z-3u+v=0 \quad (2$$
$$x = x_s+mt;\ y = y_s+nt;\ z_s = z+t$$
$$x = mz+a;\ y = nz+b \qquad \frac{u-a}{m}=\frac{y-b}{n}=\frac{z}{1}$$
$$y^2\ (x+c)^2+y^2 = 4a-4a\sqrt{(x-c)^2+y^2}+(x-c)^2$$
$$\lim_{x\to 0}\left(\frac{1}{x}-\frac{1}{e^x-1}\right)=\lim_{x\to 0}\frac{e^x-1-x}{x(e^x-1)}=\frac{1}{2}$$
$$y'=(\ln u)'\ (\sin x)'=\frac{1}{u}\ \cos x =\frac{\cos x}{\sin x}= \cot x$$
$$\int dx = \lim_{\lambda \to 0\Delta}\int f(x)dx + \lim_{\lambda \to 0}\int f(x)dx \quad \int f(x)$$
$$\lim_{x\to 0}\frac{4x}{\tan(\pi(2+x))} = \{\frac{0}{0}\}= \lim_{x\to 0}\frac{4x}{\tan 2\pi x}=\frac{2}{\pi}$$
$$\sum x_i^2+b\sum x_i =\sum x_iy_i,\ a\sum x_i+bn =\sum y_i.$$
$$y=\pi-x;\ x\to \pi,\ y\to 0$$
$$\sin 3x = \sin 3(p-y)= \sin(3p-3p)=\sin 3y$$

From your perspective, if you earn $50,000 of income at your job, and you are, let's say, in a 30 percent tax bracket, your tax is $15,000. Simple math, isn't it?

Through the eyes of my dad, a CPA, he would say maybe you owe $15,000. His job was to find every legal loophole, deduction, credit, and offset to reduce your income and ultimately reduce your tax.

How many other countless industries and situations can you apply this philosophy to? How many other times did you see or hear something on TV or the radio or read something in a magazine, newspaper, or online that made sense to you at the time, so much so that the outcome seemed so predictable, only to be shocked by the ultimate outcome?

1 + 1 = 2 MAYBE.
Can you say?

* The Trump versus Clinton election
* Rodney King verdict
* O. J. Simpson verdict
* The dot-com era
* The real-estate bubble
* Maybe your own tax return

You may have your own list where, in your mind, the outcome of a situation or event was easily predictable—or so you thought, based on what you were being spoon-fed by outside influences. It's very hard for the average person to separate the wheat from the chaff. In the hands of a well-trained attorney, PR firm, media or financial adviser with great charts and graphs, what appears to be 100 percent predictable can not only shock you but also shock an entire world.

So you may be asking yourself, what does this have to do with my investments, 401(k), and future retirement?

Great question. My goal in writing this book is to demonstrate to you that Wall Street and all those other countless talking heads you watch on TV, listen to on the radio, or read online, in your newspaper, or in magazines, books, or journals have one job, and that's to convince you that $1 + 1 = 2$ always and that if you simply take their advice, the outcome is predictable. How's that worked for you so far?

Learn this rule well. Learn how to defend yourself from falling prey to it and its dangerous consequences. As an investor, if you learn it well, it can help you make better investment decisions with your 401(k)s, IRAs, 403(b)s, and other investments. With a little bit of luck, lots of discipline and patience, you may make it to that beach and lounge chair in retirement after all.

When I first meet with a new prospective client, all that the client wants to focus on is our portfolios' historical rates of return. I can fully understand that based on where the average investor is coming from and how little else he or she pays attention to other than the returns. I get it: clients want to compare their most recent returns to ours as if that tells the entire story. Sadly, many investors believe it does.

In their minds, it's as if they are saying to themselves, "If ours portfolios performed better than theirs, then they may feel they should change advisers and have us manage their portfolio." On the other hand, if they happened to outperform us, then in their minds, they are obviously thinking that they are doing a better job, and they would see no reason to make a change.

1 + 1 = 2 Maybe?

If you are a typical investor, you may be saying to yourself, "That makes sense to me." I guess on the surface it does, but understanding investing and portfolio design requires a focus on more than simply last year's returns.

Although I can't deny that we all want a great rate of return, the rate of return alone only tells part of the story. I believe all investors benefit by having very diversified portfolios. Further, I believe diversification should be found not just in the US markets but internationally as well. In addition, you want to be sure that you are not assuming any unnecessary risk and, more importantly, you understand how much risk you are taking on and the consequences of it.

So what does risk and diversification have to do with our portfolios underperforming a prospective client's portfolio?

First of all, rates of return vary from year to year. Even though our portfolios may have underperformed your portfolio for a year or two, does that mean you have a better portfolio?

Let's assume for the last two years, you may have out earned our portfolios. The real question you should be asking yourself is why:

1. You probably have a higher equity allocation and are taking on way more risk than you are aware of. Even though that riskier allocation has produced a higher return, without a systematic rebalancing strategy, free from emotional decisions when the market swings the other way, then sadly, you will understand the consequences of only focusing on achieving higher returns. Then you will learn the meaning of "risk-related return" the hard way. Everyone talks about a portfolio's upward returns, but few stop and do the same on the way down. We do. We believe you need to have a strategy

to protect your downside position, other than simply market timing. That's what we do, and it starts and ends with the design, implementation, and management of the specific allocation we create for you, which will help you achieve the return you want while keeping the volatility in the specific range that you can live with.

2. You may not accept this, but you probably just got lucky. There's no denying that luck can play a part in everyone's portfolio from time to time. As an adviser, I would much rather be disciplined and adhere to an academic philosophy than rely on luck. The hard part for many investors is knowing the difference.

3. Your portfolio wasn't as diversified as ours. Now I am sure you are saying, "Who cares? I beat your return."

    Let me share with you what's probably going on by giving you a real-life example.

    If you recall, 2014 was not a great year for the US market except for the S&P 500/US large caps, which were up around 14 percent. Some of our portfolios may only have a maximum of 10 percent in US large-cap stocks in our most aggressive allocations. That means if you were a fifty-fifty investor with a $100,000 portfolio, you would have 50 percent, or $50,000, in equities and 50 percent, or $50,000, in fixed income. Our fifty-fifty allocation only has 4 percent in US large caps, which means of your $50,000 in equities, only $2,000 is in the US large caps, which yielded 14 percent. In this example, only $2,000 out of your entire $50,000 earned 14 percent. Now you can at least understand why, in 2014, our portfolios were flat across most allocations.

On the other hand, if you made money in 2014, I believe you were not only lucky but ill-advised because you clearly had most of your money in the S&P 500/large caps and didn't have a diversified portfolio. You may be saying to yourself, "So what? My portfolio made money, and yours didn't."

In my opinion, if you made money in 2014, you may want to consider firing your adviser. Why would I fire my adviser, you ask, if he made me money when everyone else didn't? The reason why you may want to fire your adviser is because he or she had way too much of your money in any one US asset class—US large caps just happened to be the only US asset class to make money that year. Luck or skill—you tell me. If it was luck, and I don't know anything else you can call it, do you really want your adviser to believe in luck as a strategy, or do you want to use sound academic principles?

So in this case, being globally diversified as we are did not help us for 2014, but I wouldn't change a thing in our portfolio design. The problem is, you probably wouldn't either, and that's actually the bigger issue.

History shows us time and time again that past performance is no guarantee of future performance. I would always recommend a well-diversified portfolio over having most of your money in any one particular asset class.

There's always a reason why one portfolio out earns another portfolio. The real trick is knowing why.

Successful Investing Is a Lot Like Religion and Faith

• • •

NOW THAT I HAVE YOUR attention—and if you haven't tossed the book across the room yet—let me explain what I mean. I am not talking about any specific religion. I am referring to simply having faith. When I say faith, I am referring to something that you believe in and can rely and lean on when the going gets tough in your life. Let me give you an example.

Life has a way of knocking us all down from time to time. It can be a divorce, an unexpected death of a spouse or the unthinkable death of a child, a drug or alcohol addiction, or the loss of a job. You get the idea. No matter who we are or how much money we have or don't have, tragedy can and does strike all walks of life from the bus driver to the famous movie star. The real question is this: When we are suddenly faced with this crisis, how do we handle it?

I believe we all have personally witnessed others who have been faced with many of these life challenges and have witnessed people who have handled the same situations so differently.

Quite often the families that have a religious background, what I call "faith," will still have the same emotional issues to deal with and work through, but their faith will help them surmount these stressful times without a dysfunctional and destructive response and by not destroying their lives and others around them as well.

We also have either personally observed or known of others who have had similar crises but had no religious background or faith, and they handled the situation so differently. They may have turned to alcohol, drugs, gambling, isolation, or worse. Their lack of faith had serious consequences affecting them and others.

So what does this have to do with investing?

I believe if you have taken the time to develop a true philosophy about investing—one based on sound academic principles over time, not just a hunch or what one talking head says on TV or chasing last year's winners—this faith will help you avoid making dangerous emotional and often self-destructive decisions about your portfolio.

On the other hand, **if you really haven't taken the time to develop a true investing philosophy, one that you can live with in both good and bad times, you may be in danger of using a follow-the-leader investing approach.** That's simply buying things that everyone is talking about that may have had a good track record and following the same process when you sell. If this describes your approach to investing, you may be in real danger of blowing up your retirement in the future. Sadly enough, this group comprises the largest segment of investors and Wall Street, and the media makes it even worse by yelling, "Fire," "Sell, sell, sell," "Run to cash," or "The danger has passed, and it's okay to get back into the market again." TV, radio, and other media are great at creating the stampede both away from the market and back to it as well.

My hope is that this book will help you develop a simple philosophy about investing that will guide you throughout your pre- and post-retirement years. It should also help you avoid getting trampled to death as the pundits shout, "Sharks! Get out of the water!" as you wait patiently on the water's edge for the all safe whistle to get back in.

One of the Most Important Questions You Need to Ask Yourself about Investing

• • •

WHAT DO YOU BELIEVE ABOUT MARKETS AND WHERE RETURNS REALLY COME FROM?

WHAT I AM SIMPLY ASKING you is this: Do you believe the stock market is predictable? Do you believe all those talking heads on TV and radio who tell us what to buy and sell really know the future? After all, isn't that what they are really saying?

Most people would be very quick to say, "Of course, I don't." Given the opportunity to do a portfolio analysis on your investments, I would probably find that if you are like most investors, the analysis would tell a completely different story.

If most investors don't think the stock market is predictable, then explain to me why most investors come into my office with portfolios that are incredibly under diversified? Quite often, a very large percentage of their US equity is mostly if not entirely invested in the S&P 500/large-cap stocks. Worse yet, they have little if any money in US small or small-value companies, let alone any investments overseas.

You say and even believe that you don't think the stock market is predictable, but what you may actually be doing with your investments could shout out a completely different story.

If that's you, here's an easy fix.

Just stop saying you don't think the market is predictable, or change what you are doing.

All I am asking you to do is be sure what you are saying is truly in alignment with what you are doing.

You may not think that you have an investment philosophy or strategy, but the way your portfolio is designed says at least your adviser does. Don't you think it would be a good idea for both you and your adviser to be on the same page and have the same philosophy?

It would be almost comical when people bantered around investment conversation and advice every day to each other—if the consequences weren't so dire. People are so quick to repeat what they heard today about the stock market, and they have zero understanding of how what they heard will or will not affect their personal portfolios.

1 + 1 = 2 Maybe?

Let me give you an easy example. Someone may walk into my office while the S&P 500 or the Dow is struggling and say that the market and the economy are having a difficult time lately. When I ask that person to define for me what he or she calls "the market," it's clear to me that he or she believes the stock market is simply the S&P 500 and the Dow without paying any attention to the additional US asset classes, let alone the rest of the world's investing opportunities.

How can anyone hope to achieve "market returns" when all he or she focuses on are the S&P 500/large-cap stocks or the Dow, or when the investor only invests in the United States?

On the other hand, I would define "the market" completely differently. My definition would also include markets outside the United States, not simply the S&P 500 and the Dow.

When you examine our portfolios, our global view of investing and diversification is clearly reflected in them and their design. The portfolios that we tailor for you look very different, with much more worldwide diversification than what most people have when they come into our office.

If you recall, we said earlier that when many people come to our office and allow us to do a portfolio analysis, we tend to find most of their US funds are in US large caps/S&P 500. Many may have as much as 60 percent or more of their US investments in US large caps. In contrast, many of our portfolios will have less than 10 percent of all US equity in US large caps. This allows us to have more of an investor's funds still available to be invested in more diversified ways in the United States and overseas. We also find these same people who may have some money invested overseas also have most if not all of their money in the overseas equivalent of US large caps, ignoring international diversification.

A Few Simple Investing Rules to Follow

• • •

THESE RULES ARE SIMPLE BUT not easy to follow. Probably you could say the same thing about dieting. The rules for losing weight are to eat less and move more.

I believe the rules to investing are equally easy to understand but just as hard to follow.

Own equities. I believe equities are the greatest way to create wealth known to mankind. When you invest in equities, you are investing in the free enterprise system. Even though half the civilized population loves their iPhones, I am fairly confident somewhere in the free world, there is some company trying to invent a new cell phone, other gadget or product that hopes to one-up the competition, and if successful, they will be handsomely rewarded for their effort. Maybe it will happen, maybe it won't, but when this no-name company is ready to go public, the world will decide if its new product or invention is worth investing in. This story plays itself out thousands of times a year throughout the free world. It did with Apple, Facebook, and Google, just to mention a few. As long as there are people with dreams and new visions, there will be equities to invest in and people who profit by wisely doing so. Of course, the real secret is determining which ones to invest in and which ones to pass on.

Be diversified. Invest all over the world and in many different asset classes. We live in a global economy, and long gone are the days when a prudent investor can say he or she wants market returns and still have all or most of his or her investments in America.

Have a systematic plan to rebalance on the highs and lows that will take emotion out of the equation. When I ask investors when and why they rebalance, it's apparent they don't have a true understanding or a systematic plan to do so. Most wing it, at best. Rebalancing is not as much about your return as it is being sure that your portfolio doesn't drift from your specific allocation preference to a more risky one. Let's assume you choose to be a fifty-fifty investor. That's 50 percent in equities of some kind and 50 percent in fixed income and bonds. You chose this fifty-fifty allocation because the risk and volatility were explained to you, and as much as you wanted to attempt to earn a higher rate of return, you weren't comfortable with a higher equity allocation and taking on more risk.

Let's assume your 50 percent equity position goes up 10 percent. Do you rebalance back to fifty-fifty? Of course not. You just earned 10 percent, but suddenly you have drifted to a fifty-forty five allocation. Luckily again, your 55 percent equity continues to inch its way up, and again, it gains another 10 percent. Now you have drifted to an approximately 60 percent equity and 40 percent fixed income allocation. Do you rebalance back to your original fifty-fifty? Heck no. You're invincible and on autopilot, and greed has its hooks deeply embedded in you. Simply put, which allocation—fifty-fifty, sixty-forty, or seventy-thirty—is riskier and has much more volatility? A seventy-thirty, of course. Eventually, the market drops, and you get hammered and look for someone to blame.

How could this significant, needless loss have been avoided? Simple. If you'd had a systematic strategy to rebalance, free from emotion, your portfolio wouldn't have drifted to seventy-thirty in the first place. For example, I recommend you review the portfolio quarterly; if the portfolio allocation has drifted by more than 5 percent up or down, I would advise to rebalance back to the target allocation. Of course, you don't have to use a 5 percent per quarter strategy, but committing to having a number and a system takes the emotion and guesswork out of it.

Be sure all your investments aren't highly correlated the same. When you design and construct your portfolio, you want to be sure that all your investments are not highly correlated alike. You don't want your entire portfolio to move in the same direction at the same time.

Pay attention to fees. Size matters, especially in the fees that you are paying. One of the fastest ways you may be able to increase your returns is by reducing the fees you are paying. If you have no idea what you are paying in true overall fees, how can you go shopping for something with fewer fees? You can't!

It still surprises me that people continue to say, "I don't worry about the fees, I just look at the bottom line." They also may say something like, "I'm happy with my returns. I made 9 percent last year." The truth is, they may have made a lot more than 9 percent, but that's what they were able to keep after all the fees came out. They may have made 12 percent but had 3 percent in fees. If that's the case, try to find an investment replacement in the same sector with fewer fees. It really amazes me that most people know what they paid per gallon of gas last week to the penny but really have no idea what they are paying in investment fees. That's simply not okay anymore!

There are many different fees you may be paying, and some you may not even know exist. Of course, there are the **adviser's fees,** but those are usually found on your statements. There are additional fees that are almost impossible to find, and, if you believe Wall Street, they don't even matter. **Some of these fees include the expense ratio on mutual funds, 12b-1 fees, portfolio turnover fees, and front- and back-end loads.**

If you are saying to yourself that you have never heard of any of these fees and have no idea if you are paying any of them, that's a problem.

Don't gamble on hot picks or anything trendy. Buying trendy clothes or electronics is great, but try to avoid it when investing. I know doing so can be fun and feel like the cool thing to do, but you need to know the difference between gambling or speculating with your money and prudent investing that has the broad backing of academics to support your investment decisions.

Be disciplined, and stay the course. "Delbar" is a research group out of Boston that tracks investors' behaviors and results. "Delbar" finds that the average investor not only significantly underperforms the market but does so often because he or she changes and tinkers with their portfolio about every three years. Think about that. The average person reading this (and yes, I know, that's not you—you're not average) is more committed to wearing his or her worn-down shoes than in sticking with the investment decisions they made less than 4 years ago. How scary is that?

Avoid market timing. Market timing is getting in the market because you believe that it's a great time to invest or getting out because you think it's wise. Market timing can destroy a retirement. If this is your philosophy, the problem is that you have to be right twice every time you do this—once when you get out and once when you decide to get back in. If you time the market, for example, ten times a year, that's ten times getting out of the market and ten times eventually getting back in. That's twenty times per year, and if you are going to do that as a philosophy over a forty-five-year investing career, you only have to be right about nine hundred times. Good luck with that! Studies show some of the market's greatest upticks immediately follow some of the biggest drops. Most people who market-time miss all or most of that upward bounce.

Remember that past performance isn't any guarantee of future performance. This is so widely understood that when I teach retirement classes at some of the local universities, I will start saying this well-known-but-not-believed phrase and, without fail, the entire class will all jump in and complete it. You may be saying it to yourself right now. Study after study shows a manager's past performance has no correlation with his or her future performance, but **the average investor still wants to look in the rearview mirror to pick investments.** *Don't do it!*

Remember that no one can predict the future. And if they could, would they really tell you? Let me repeat this: no one can predict what's going to happen in the stock market today, tomorrow, next week, or next year. No TV or radio host shouting what to buy, no newspaper, Internet website, or your smart friend. No one!

Know how to measure volatility in your portfolio. Not all risk is the same. You shouldn't take any more risk than necessary to achieve the return you are after. **One of the most important numbers you should know concerning your portfolio is its** *standard deviation.* In simple terms, it's a number that each stock and mutual fund has. When you combine all these different stocks and funds into a comprehensive portfolio, they all interact with each other, and this creates a new standard deviation for the entire portfolio. The higher the standard deviation, the higher the expected return may be in good times, and it reveals how much downward volatility you should expect in bad times.

I like to say that this number is to a financial adviser what a PSA is to an urologist. Anyone who has ever had a bout with prostate cancer waits for nothing more than to hear the PSA number from his doctor. This number tells him what his medical future looks like. Knowing your standard deviation is that critical to your long term financial health. It may possibly reduce your standard deviation and either keep your return the same or possibly increase it. Do you know your standard deviation? If you knew that your standard deviation was too high in 2007, and you reduced it, you might not have lost nearly as much in the 2008 crash.

All I Want to Do Is Beat the S&P 500

• • •

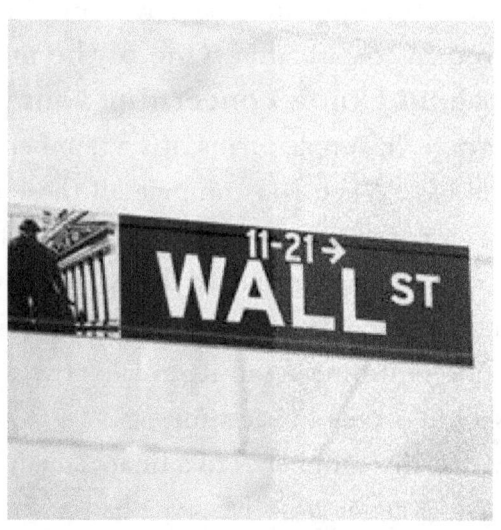

TODAY, EVERY INVESTOR'S MAIN FOCUS is trying to beat the S&P 500, as if the S&P 500 is the holy grail of investing—or that's at least what the media has convinced us we should want as our investing goal. Perhaps that may explain why so many portfolios we review are so heavily invested in it.

Every mutual fund's ultimate trophy to hold high on January 1 is one reflecting that the fund beat the S&P 500. What a powerful advertisement or headline to lure you to roll the dice and invest with the fund, hoping it can beat the S&P 500 again next year. What makes the fund so special? Nothing.

Stop and ask yourself a simple question.

Are the fund managers reporting history, what has happened last year, or what will happen next year? Last year, of course. Not one of these firms that have graced the covers of countless magazines, newsletters, and other media, bragging about beating the S&P 500 last year, will ever dare to make a prediction for which one of their many funds will do it again this year.

Imagine if you were a meteorologist, and your boss came in and said, "If your weather forecast isn't 100 percent accurate today, you will lose your job." Wow, that's a lot of pressure, especially living in Cleveland. That task sounds impossible to do, doesn't it? Maybe not. How about if the boss continued and said, "Today, I want your forecast to simply report on yesterday's weather." Now the task got much easier, didn't it?

So how does Wall Street convince us that it is omniscient and that all you have to do is follow its advice and success is almost assured?

The Law of Large Numbers

• • •

IF YOU ARE A MUTUAL-FUND family that has literally hundreds of different funds to choose from, how do you convince investors to buy your funds? Beat the S&P 500 last year, and investors will beat a path to your door.

If the goal is to simply beat the S&P 500, isn't there a 50 percent chance of success? You either beat it or you don't. Let's assume your family of funds has five hundred different funds for investors to choose from. I am not a mathematician, but even I know that if there are five hundred funds, and I have a 50 percent chance, I would expect anywhere between two hundred and three hundred or maybe more of these five hundred funds to beat the S&P 500. No magic or special skill there—just the law of large numbers. The real magic is how easily these mutual funds can share last year's results to investors and you assume that these funds managers are so special that all you will need to do to achieve financial success is invest in last year's winners.

Who cares that for years we have been told over and over again that…get ready, I know you are already saying the words to yourself: **"Past performance is no guarantee of future performance."** Yes, but you say this time is different, isn't it? No, it's not!

Stop trying to beat the market, and start trying to achieve market returns.

Stop Trying To Beat The Market

It's well documented that most money managers can't beat the S&P 500, and the ones who do rarely repeat. My goal for you would be to help you think more in terms of achieving market returns versus trying to beat the market. Again, Delbar is a company that tracks investors' results and behaviors, and its research has indicated that most investors underperform the market. In addition, **there is a big difference between what the specific investment earns and what the investor earns.** What did I say? You read that right—most investors don't earn what the market yields. It's as if the market knocks on your front door and says, "We are going to yield eight percent this year. Would you like to earn eight percent?" To which you say, "No, I am fine earning less." Really!

How does this happen?

It's mostly due to investor behaviors.

Didn't I Hear This Somewhere Before?

I know we reviewed these points before, but they are so critical to an investor's success that they are worth repeating.

Research continues to show that most investors change all or part of their portfolios every three years. Like I said earlier, most people wear their shoes twice as long as they stick with their investment strategies. If properly done, your specific investment strategy should help guide you throughout your entire life as an investor and keep you from making these needless and frequent changes.

Track-record investing. Even though we know the rules, research continues to show that most investors get sucked in and use the past performance of an investment heavily to influence their future investment decisions.

Stock picking. Too many investors spend countless hours trying to find magical stocks that they believe will forever change their portfolio for the better. Stop looking. I can't argue the fact that anyone can get lucky from time to time, but trying to find a magic stock is not how an investor should design a long-term investment strategy.

Market timing. Here's another area I know most investors would agree with but have a very difficult time living with. Market timing is simply getting into (or out of) the market because you think this is a great time to do so. The problem with market timing is you need to be right twice every time you do it. You need to be right when you get out of the market and right again when you buy back in. I said this earlier but it is so important that it is necessary to repeat. Let's assume you rely on this philosophy as an investor and that throughout any one year there can be as many as ten times a year you would exit and reenter. That's twenty decisions you need to be right with in that year alone. Times forty-five years as an investor, you only need to be right nine hundred times. Market timing is dangerous and destructive, so please avoid it.

These are all investor behavioral issues and not actual portfolio issues, but clearly your behavior will affect your portfolio results.

US Large Caps, Aisle 4

• • •

TO THE AVERAGE INVESTOR, INVESTING is nothing more than shopping for things that you believe are a good investment.

Sounds easy enough. Duh, you say—but not so quickly. Really. What do you think the average investor looks for when making investment decisions? As much as I rail against it, I still find that 90 percent of clients tell me that they look at how well it has done in the past. They pay zero attention to the standard deviation of their portfolio, fees, turnover, and/or overlap, nor do they know the importance of these terms.

It's as if people think that by filling up their shopping cart with good investments, whatever those may be, they are assured a great portfolio return. That's no truer than saying if you pick up good food at the market, you are assured a great meal. Who needs a stinking recipe? Who cares about using way too much salt? I hope you are not part of the crowd saying, "I don't see a problem yet."

Here's The Problem.
No one has just one stock or one mutual fund. At least, I hope not.

As you fill your shopping cart with investments, do you have the slightest idea how the different investments will all work together? Are they all highly correlated the same? I hope not; how non-correlated are they or should they be? Do you know the total amount of combined fees, overlap, and turnover you have in the entire portfolio? If you look for international investments, and I hope you do, what countries will you look for, and which are the ones to avoid? How will you determine the proper percentage of each? And what about rebalancing? These are just some of the big problems that most investors don't pay a lot of attention to. Do you?

When we design and engineer a portfolio, it is more than simply the sum of all investments. A good portfolio is engineered and designed to work together with the tens of thousands of holdings from all over the world in many different asset classes that comprise a diversified portfolio. This is what is missing from and is critical to most do-it-yourself investors and their portfolios.

How do you make your investment decisions? When I ask average investors how they make investment decisions, 99 percent will say to me that they look at what it earned last year and what it has averaged over the last five and ten years. For most people, that's it.

In my opinion, those are two of the most worthless pieces of information you could look at when making your investment choices.

Recall what I shared earlier:

1. Past performance has no bearing on future returns.
2. According to "Delbar" most people tinker or change their investments every three years, so how does a five- or ten-year average even help you?

Remember that the published five- and ten-year returns only go to the few disciplined investors who don't change their investments over that five- and ten-year time period. If you are average, and I hope you aren't, you aren't even earning what the investment has yielded. Most investors don't.

There's normally an incredible difference between what the investments itself has earned and what you, the investor, earns. The investment is committed for a long term and disciplined, but most investors aren't and can't say the same thing. That's why we said earlier that while most investors are busy trying to beat the market, they usually underperform it time and time again.

I believe an investor should be more concerned about the following questions:

1. What is this investment designed to earn (average) over the next ten to twenty years?
2. What is my expected downside risk that I should expect to lose occasionally if the market goes south? (And it will over time, so knowing this number is critical.)

The financial industry tries at all costs to stay away from the word "guarantee." Many advisers I know have gotten into trouble from the mere mention of that word. Regulators go to painstaking efforts to be sure advisers don't cite returns in literature or on their websites or marketing materials. They want to protect investors from being led to believe past performance somehow has any bearing on future returns. **The sad thing is, that's exactly what most investors rely on.** Here's something I can guarantee and will sleep well knowing: no regulator will knock on my door because I used the following statement: "There will be periods of time your portfolio may perform way better than you ever thought it would, and you will think I am a genius. And, of course, there will be times that your portfolio will underperform your expectations, and you may wonder if I even know what I am doing."

Portfolio ups and downs are natural, common, and to be expected. When the leaves fall off your trees in October and November, you don't call your landscaper and scream at him to cut them down. There is a season for everything, and your investments are no different.

Here is the problem: if you are like most investors, you have no understanding of the actual downside potential of your portfolio. Why should you? No one ever decided to explain it to you while painting a pretty picture of the average returns that you may never see.

So, to me, the most critical piece of information you should focus on is finding a specific percentage of loss in any year in your portfolio that you can tolerate and not make any changes other than to rebalance your portfolio. Once we can isolate that number, we can back into the expected rate of return you can expect based on the amount of volatility you can live with. This is a realistic way to be sure you are designing a portfolio specifically built for your personal risk tolerance.

For me to be an effective adviser, I need you to say the actual percentage, out loud. I want to avoid words like "conservative" and "moderate," as they mean different things to everyone.

Take this easy test with your spouse or a friend to determine if you and your financial adviser are speaking the same language.

Let's assume everyone is in the same moderate portfolio. You hear on the news that the stock market has gone down 30 percent. Write down, without sharing your answer, what percentage you would expect your portfolio to go down by as well.

Now compare the answers. I'll bet each person has a different percentage of loss. How can that be? We all are in the same moderate portfolio. We all experience the same 30 percent stock-market loss.

But we all have a different definition of "moderate."

That's why I don't use industry language to determine your risk tolerance. That's why I asked you to tell me what percentage you can live with as an occasional downside; then we do the math against your portfolio, and see if you still feel the same.

Currently, most clients and advisers aren't even speaking the same language. How can we even hope to get on the same page with our expectations?

Education Is Key

• • •

OFTEN WHEN POTENTIAL CLIENTS COME in, they will be honest and tell me that they have changed advisers four or five times over the last twenty years, and the outcome always seems to be the same. They wonder out loud: "What makes me different?"

I will patiently and politely retrace all that they have done over the last twenty years with the other advisers. I will listen carefully to what strategy they choose to use, what they did when there was volatility in the market, and what their thoughts are on rebalancing, fees, and risk. Most of the time, I get a blank stare, and they recite what sounds good, and they hope it makes them sound like they know what they are talking about. Ultimately, I smile and say, "It looks like the only common denominator with all the past advisers is you!"

Quite often, I believe, the investors are a big part of the problem. They get bombarded with way too much information and have no investment philosophy, but they know that they want higher returns and will buy and sell as often as necessary to achieve them.

Until investors get a handle on what they believe about the market and where returns come from, until they come up with a philosophy they can live with in both good and bad times, and until they understand how to measure risk and fees, they simply are stuck with making emotional and dangerous investment decisions.

Our feelings, right or wrong, will ultimately drive our investment decisions.

If I, as a wealth coach, can't help you get clear on where you believe returns come from and help you develop a philosophy about returns and the market, I am destined to be the next adviser who will also disappoint you.

I can't stop anyone from watching or listening to any investment TV or radio show or reading any magazine or newspaper. This financial pornography floods the airwaves, newsstands, mailboxes, and computer screens and poisons the minds of many investors. This overload of information plants seeds of frustration and discontentment in their minds about their portfolios. If you are not careful, the next phone call you may make may be to your adviser with instructions to sell and buy based on what you heard on TV or read.

Coaching Makes The Difference

• • •

OFTEN, ANYONE TRYING TO ACCOMPLISH something meaningful and significant needs a relationship with a coach. Coaching helps get you to the next level to achieve the accomplishments you seek. Most great athletes who are at the top of their game have many different kinds of coaches. Great business icons also use coaches. Today, many people use life coaches. A good coach will help you achieve what you say you want to attain. A great coach can help bring an unemotional perspective to the task. A great coach will hold you accountable and not accept your excuses. A great coach will tell you what you need to hear but may not want to listen to.

I Can't Eat Any More

• • •

Have you ever gone on a vacation and stayed at one of those fancy hotels that have an incredibly overpriced Sunday buffet? After you decide to spend fifty-nine dollars on a brunch, you walk into a ballroom that is filled with food from wall to wall. Where do you start? There are way too many choices. All you really wanted was breakfast.

It has become that way with investing information. There are more financial TV and radio shows than anyone would think is even possible. Worse yet, they air 24-7. Don't get me started with how much worthless information is packaged online, or on TV or radio as education. It is nothing more than a commercial or a fancy sales pitch just to sell you something.

Today you are being convinced to manage your own money online and use the many fun online tools and research. How hard can it be?

Research has shown that people with online trading accounts needlessly trade and speculate way more often than those without online trading accounts.

In addition, the newest trend are the so-called "Robo advisers." You simply turn your financial future over to an online electronic robot, and it does all the investing for you. Now that sounds scary. I don't know about you but I am certainly not comfortable handing over my entire portfolio over to a computer. Are you?

Estate Planning 101

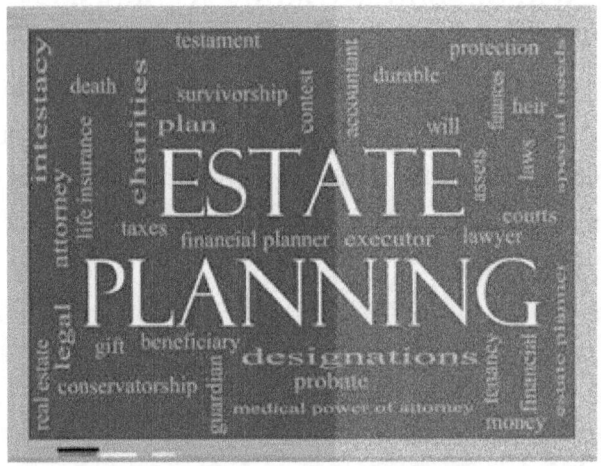

THE BEST FINANCIAL PLAN MAY be rendered worthless if you don't have a good estate plan in place. I need to say from the outset that I am not an attorney and that none of what I am about to share is intended to be legal advice in any way. The purpose of this section is to simply share with you what my professional career has exposed me to and to offer twenty-five years of experience in dealing with both attorneys and people's estates. I would recommend that if I say anything that hits home, seek legal advice.

What's an estate?

Everything you own is your estate, including your home, cars, stocks, bonds, mutual funds, cash, jewelry, and lawn mower.

What's an estate plan?

An estate plan is created to handle your possessions upon your death or disability.

You may be surprised to learn that many people do nothing and don't even have a will. They assume that it will all take care of itself or that their spouses will get everything anyway after they die. That may be true, but many spouses may learn the hard lesson after the fact and an array of different circumstances. Let me walk you through some different situations, terms, ideas, and strategies you may want to explore with your attorney.

I have a will. What else do I need?

Having an up-to-date will drafted by an attorney from the state you live in is a great start. So many people I meet with tell me that they don't have a will, or if they do, it's very old and outdated, or it's from another state. You always want to be sure that it is current and reflects your current wishes. It should be drafted by an attorney and be based on the law in the state you call your primary residence. A will isn't a valid and/or working document until after you die. Be sure you and your spouse and beneficiaries know where the original document is because often your descendants need to file the original with the court.

Your will is your ticket to probate.

Many people want to avoid probate and have their estates pass to beneficiaries as fast as possible, with the fewest delays and least amount of expense. Many families have their wills drafted specifically to avoid probate without understanding that the wills they had drawn up may force them into the very long probate process they sought to avoid. You may want to talk to your attorney about having a living trust rather than a conventional will as your main estate-planning document. Simply put, a revocable living trust normally will help you pass your estate to the beneficiaries without all the delay and added cost of probate.

Many families don't want to give the entire estate to a child all at once. If you find yourself not comfortable passing it all at once what took you a lifetime to achieve, talk to your attorney about how a trust may be able to do a better job for you. One of the unique things about a trust is that you can design a custom lifelong distribution for beneficiaries paid out over time versus all at once.

I would recommend you have both a *power of attorney for health care* and a *durable power of attorney*. Many families I talk to are still working, and their largest investment often is their 401(k)/403(b) or IRA. These same families are often shocked when I tell them that if they don't have a durable power of attorney and the family member with the 401(k), IRA, or 403(b) becomes sick and is not able to function or conduct business, the caretaker spouse won't able to get a penny from the 401(k), IRA, or 403(b).

Well, that's not entirely true. If you find yourself in this position, you will need to hire an attorney, go to the court, and apply to be the guardian of your spouse so you can access these accounts. This can be an expensive and time-consuming process. Having a durable power of attorney can prevent this outcome. Of course, if you are the beneficiary, you will inherit these funds without a durable power of attorney. But that, of course, only happens at death.

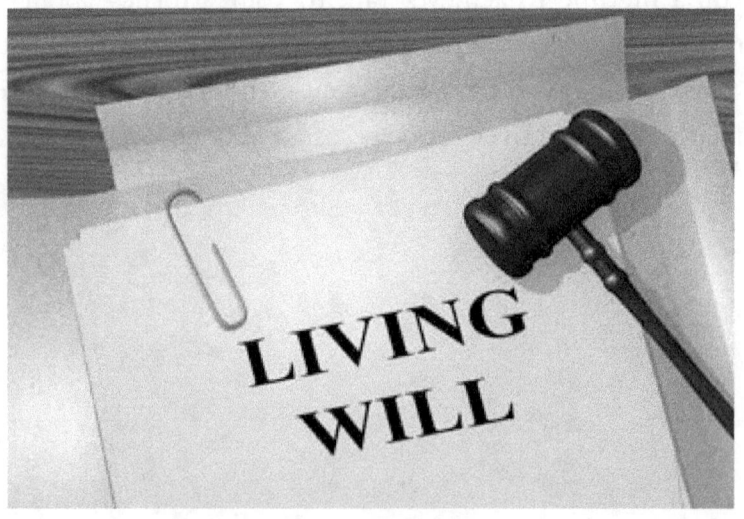

A *living will* is called many different things in different states, but it helps your family know your personal wishes concerning life and death and what kind of medical heroics you are willing to be subjected to. This simply makes it easier for the family, at a highly emotional time, to feel that they are not imposing their beliefs and decisions about prolonging your care. It further helps the family avoid getting into an emotional war over your deathbed. I have seen the aftermath of situations where the family didn't have this critical document to guide them and was forced to make decisions concerning the care of a loved one as the end drew closer. Often siblings took different positions. The damage this causes to the fabric of the family may never be able to be repaired.

Many people think that you must have a lot of money to be bothered with setting up an estate plan.

That's a common misconception.

The decision to set up an estate plan should not be solely based on how much money you have or don't have but, more importantly, also on how you feel about the money you do have and that your family will inherit. It's kind of the opposite of what you may think as to who may benefit more by setting up an estate plan. The families who are lucky enough to have a lot of money can actually afford to go through the more expensive probate process, while the families that are less financially well-off may benefit more in protecting every dollar from probate. If I now have you thinking more about your estate plan and wanting to talk to your attorney, that's a good thing.

But what if you end up in a nursing home?

If you don't invest some time and energy thinking about what could happen financially to you and your family if you end up in a nursing home, "it will probably end badly."

It's paradoxical that the idea of living a long life appeals to everyone, but the idea of getting old doesn't appeal to anyone.
—Andy Rooney

We all know that life isn't infinite and the grim reaper of death, disabilities and despair won't be defeated. And while modern medicine has made huge strides in fighting heart disease, diabetes, and cancer, we all still die.

The lucky ones will die suddenly. Here today, living life to the fullest…gone tomorrow. Sad for our loved ones, but much better than dying a slow death where our health declines daily, limited to a wheelchair, incapable of recalling our children's names, and needing assistance to visit the bathroom.

Depressing…isn't it? That's life.

As a society, we are living longer. That is a good thing, but that also means our money must last longer. It means that eventually we will become weak and likely to need help with those things we only want to do for ourselves (custodial care).

Here are some interesting statistics:

- If you reach age sixty-five, there's a 70 percent chance you'll need custodial care.
- The average nursing-home stay is almost three years.
- The average nursing-home cost is $70,000 a year.
- Nursing-home costs rise at twice the average inflation rate.
- Medicare doesn't pay for long-term care.
- Medicaid is available only after you've spent down your assets.

- Most people in nursing homes are on Medicaid, but they didn't start there.

Basically, you have three options when it comes to long-term care:

- First, you can self-insure and pay the nursing-home bill from your savings and/or investments. Perhaps you have enough money to do that. Remember…its $70,000 a year now. At 6 percent inflation, the price will double in twelve years. If you're married, and you get sick, will that leave enough money for your healthy spouse?
- Second, you can't rely on Medicaid. Why not? Most do, but that's available only after you've spent down your own money. If you're married, Medicaid kicks in when you have about $100,000 left. You don't have to sell your house, but the government may attach a lien to it after you die so that it can recoup the cost of your care.
- Third, you can buy long-term-care insurance. For many people, this is the right choice. Often we hear people say they won't buy it out of fear they'll never use it and thus waste their money. We're going to let you in on a little secret: the people who go to nursing homes with long-term care don't win the game. It's those who have long-term-care insurance but die peacefully in their sleep—healthy today…dead tomorrow—who win the game.

    When your car isn't stolen, do you regret paying auto insurance? Never feel regret for being prudent.

Long-term-care insurance can be expensive, but a few things can be done to reduce it:

1. Limit coverage to four years. Odds are very high you won't need the policy after four years. By limiting coverage to this time frame, you reduce the cost dramatically over a lifetime-benefit policy.
2. Self-insure a part of the cost. If nursing homes in your area cost $200 per day, consider coverage for $150. Be sure to study the long-term impact of not being fully insured.
3. Ask your children to pay for it. They are the ones who stand to benefit from you not spending all of their inheritance on nursing-home care.

Whatever you do…have a plan!

Closing Thoughts and Takeaways

• • •

To help investors deal with this constant explosion of too much self-serving information, I have created a series of ongoing 'Coaching" educational classes for my clients. These classes are designed to help my clients deal with this information overload and give them current and accurate academic information about the market that is delivered without emotion or trying to scare them into some kind of dysfunctional investing behavior. These classes help my clients become better informed and more educated investors. I attempt to act as a counterbalance to the endless financial misinformation and help them not overreact to the latest financial news story of the day.

For an invitation to any of my future classes in Akron, access to our line resources, or to receive our newsletter please e-mail me at **lee@leehyder.com or go to www.leehyder.com**

It's Not As Easy As It May Look.
There's more to designing a portfolio than just buying stocks and mutual funds, even if those stocks and funds have a great historical track record. (Remember what I said about track-record investing.)

Regardless of what you may think, read, or hear on TV or the radio, it's not as easy as the media or big stock-brokerage firms would like you to believe. Maybe even more important than determining what you should invest in is maintaining discipline throughout your investing career and keeping your emotions out of the equation.

Even if you could magically snap your fingers and have the perfect portfolio—if there is such a thing—if you are not truly disciplined and emotion free, you can destroy your perfect investment. I know that you are thinking, "Lee, that's not me. I am disciplined and didn't panic back in 2008."

Congratulations, but my experience tells me time and time again that if we really examine your past investment decisions, we will find countless occasions where you acted more from a place of fear or greed or on a hunch or past performance than from an academic, well-defined, disciplined strategy.

Many of you reading this may have, at one time or another, had a portfolio that was doing great, chugging along, and something happened. You panicked, and you reacted—maybe even overreacted—and changed something in your investment mix.

Of course, you wouldn't ever say that you overreacted. That change, in your mind, may appear to be very insignificant, but it was enough to alter the mix of asset classes in the portfolio, and now you may underperform the actual long-term return of the very investment you were in. Had you maybe just rebalanced the portfolio, you would have achieved the actual long-term return of the investment versus shooting yourself in your foot, just like "Delbar" says most investors do. Worse yet, you didn't even know it.

This is why most investors benefit by having a "wealth coach" versus a traditional adviser or stockbroker. Stockbrokers and many advisers do a good job selling you financial products—the flavor of the day, as I like to call them—but most advisers and brokers, I believe, act like Switzerland: they are neutral and will let you sell and buy whatever you want, even if it's not in your best interest. Even if you're rational, it's coming from a place of greed or fear. It is at these very times, when both elements are present, that it's most dangerous for you and your portfolio's long-term financial health.

When emotion sets in, a wealth coach will help you not fall prey to these self-destructive decisions. These are the times when I really earn my fees. It's not hard to sit with clients when their portfolio is up 12 percent, but it takes a different skill set on both sides of the conference table to help these same people when the portfolio is down 20 percent or more. A good coach stands for something or ultimately stands for nothing! I would rather lose a client than sit idly by and even profit by allowing them to do something that I believe is not in his or her best interest and is emotionally driven.

1 + 1 = 2 Maybe?

Regardless of what they say on TV or the radio or in what you read, a well-designed portfolio is systematically engineered with many different ingredients, like a great meal. It's simply not a collection of historically well-performing investments. The best ingredients in the kitchen can create the worst meal ever if all you do is throw them in one pot and hope it works.

CONCLUSION

• • •

MAYBE THE CONCEPT $1 + 1 = 2$ is all around us. Believing that $1 + 1 = 2$ makes our world seem more manageable and easy to understand. We want things to be simple and easy to deal with, so we can move on to the next task. We want to be able to believe what we read and see or hear on the 6:00 p.m. news. I hate to break the bad news to you, but life doesn't always work that way. There are so many groups out there today with such self-serving motivations to convince you that $1 + 1 = 2.$ You, the consumer, can't just settle for what appears to be the obvious, and you must probe deeper with your questions and conduct research so you can uncover your own "*maybe*."

I have a few simple questions?

1. Do you let past performance of an investment cloud your future investment decisions?
2. Do you think that it would be important for you to know what you are really paying in all fees, not just advisory fees?
3. Is it important to you to determine if your portfolio is too risky? And I am not just referring to the percentage of equity in your portfolio allocation.

4. Would it make more sense to manage a portfolio with a systematic strategy, with regard for when and how to rebalance, that is 100 percent free from emotion?
5. Do you think it would help you if you had an investment philosophy that is constant and something you can rely on in both good and bad times, which are 100 percent free from emotion?
6. Do you spend too much time watching and listening to TV and radio shows about investments?
7. Do you rely on a lot of online calculators, your custodian's research, financial magazines, newsletters, and websites to make your decisions?
8. Do you worry that there may not be enough money to create the retirement lifestyle you hope for?
9. Do you wish you understood investing more?
10. Has this book helped you look at investing a little differently?

If you answered yes to many of these questions, you are like the hundreds of families that have come to my office looking for answers and peace of mind.

I hope that you have enjoyed this short book; but more importantly, I hope that it spurs you to act and learn more.

If you are in the Akron, Ohio, area, we would love to meet with you and do an analysis of your portfolio, 401(k), or IRA to help give you answers and peace of mind.

If you are outside the Akron, Ohio, area, we can offer an online portfolio analysis.

For a wide variety of free reports, go to http://www.leehyder.com and click on "Free reports."

To contact me personally, e-mail lee@leehyder.com, or call 330-836-7800.

www.ingramcontent.com/pod-product-compliance
Lightning Source LLC
Chambersburg PA
CBHW061207180526
45170CB00002B/991